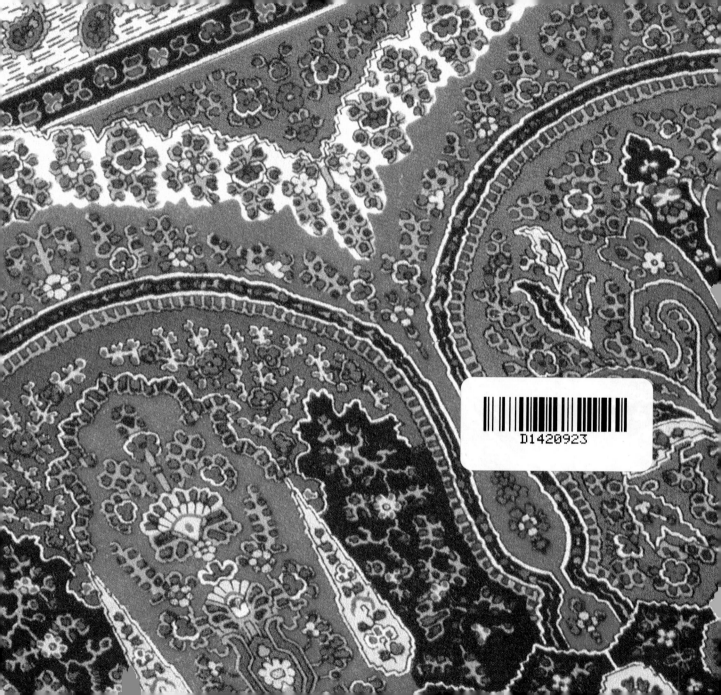

THE FIVE-MINUTE
SCARF
ARRANGER

THE FIVE-MINUTE
SCARF
ARRANGER

PIA TRYDE SANDEMAN

TIGER BOOKS INTERNATIONAL
LONDON

Conceived and produced by Breslich & Foss Ltd., London

Designed by Lisa Tai

This edition published in 1997 by
Tiger Books International PLC, Twickenham

ISBN 1-85501-895-0

Printed in China

CONTENTS

THE FIVE-MINUTE APPROACH

A scarf is a piece of flat fabric which can be any shape but it will not have been cut and joined, seamed or shaped like a piece of clothing. Scarves are an adjunct to clothes and can be used in an entirely practical way; wrapped round the neck, for example, to cover exposed skin and to keep out the cold or for decoration to add a spark of extra color or pattern to an ensemble.

Every culture has devised ways to use fabric without the need to sew and construct. An early Roman toga, an Indian sari or turban are very sophisticated ways of using fabric just as it comes off the loom. On a smaller scale a scarf made from an exquisite fabric can be used to decorate a plainer garment and is a good alternative to using masses of the same expensive fabric to make a complete piece of clothing.

In Western society scarves are more commonly worn by women though the man's tie is in effect a strip of fabric worn as a decoration. Scarves are used by women to flatter, hide, disguise and enhance; they are wrapped around or tied to every part of the body from weaving through hair to tying into a sarong skirt.

To fold a square into a triangle, take one diagonal to meet another.

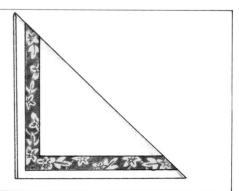

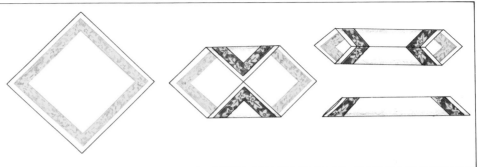

To fold a square into a long, thin rectangle, take two diagonals to meet each other at the center and fold each again.

SCARF SHAPES

It is possible to buy scarves in many different shapes but most common are squares and long, thin rectangles. A square can be folded diagonally into a triangle and further folded into a narrow strip. A long, thin rectangle is the obvious choice for wrapping round the neck or for tying round the waist or hair. Small square handkerchief scarves are useful to make into decorations and to knot simply round the neck or wrist.

FABRIC CHOICES

Scarves are made from just about every material commonly used for clothes. Wool and cashmere make soft and very warm scarves, silk and cotton, viscose and man-made mixtures are used for printed designs. Fine transparent voile and chiffon are very often used for floaty feminine scarves which weigh very little and drape gently into folds.

It is important to understand the qualities of different fabrics before trying to make arrangements with them. Stiff, crisp fabrics such as silk dupion and taffeta or plain cottons will hold their shape well where you need volume in a bow for example. Silk chiffon molds itself well to the body and drapes into soft folds but it will not make a stiff bow. Fine woolen lawn such as nuns' veiling drapes and folds well but has springiness and life. The weight of wool makes it suitable for large-scale shawls and wraps. Acrylic and acrylic mixtures are commonly used in scarves and though they look very similar to wool rarely have the subtlety of color of the real thing. The classic square scarf is usually designed with its shape in mind, often having bands or borders round the edge. They are thought out and designed as a scarf and are not simply squares cut from larger pieces of fabric. A plain silk chiffon scarf though is likely to have been cut from a larger piece of fabric and then hemmed. The hem or edge of a scarf is an important detail which can ruin the finished thing if badly done. Cheaper scarves will be machine stitched and more expensive ones will be hand hemmed. The best chiffon scarves are rolled and hemmed by hand.

Long muffler styles of scarf will have been woven on a loom individually so the edges are finished already. Often this type of scarf will have a decorative fringing or row of tassels at the two ends. Knitted jersey scarves are very common now too, miles away from the home-made look and available in a smooth fine knit of wool or wool and angora. Cotton of different colored threads is used to weave scarves or plain white cotton is dyed or printed into a never ending range of designs.

To build up a basic wardrobe of these accessories, choose a few scarves in each shape and fabric and in colors which you know flatter your skin and eye color. Select some useful neutrals too. Add a few brilliantly colorful designs for wearing in the summer or to add some excitement to monochrome outfits. The choice of scarf is a very personal thing; scarves are often given as gifts and put to the back of the drawer because they do not suit. Check what you have lurking and see if there are ideas in the next five chapters which can make use of those forgotten scarves.

BASIC SKILLS

Anyone who can tie a knot or a bow can arrange a scarf. It is important to be quite bold in the way you handle and use a scarf. If you are too tentative and over-fussy you will end up with something that has no impact. Grasp the scarf firmly and make extravagant knots and bows, wrap a scarf a few extra times, or use two together. Mean little knots and half hidden scarves look insipid and boring. You don't have to be outrageous just positive.

The basic knot you use should be a reef knot, which you can remember how to tie by saying: left over right, right over left. This leaves you with ends which lie flat and neat. To avoid always using a knot experiment with loops or use a ring (see page 15) to tie your scarves. A bow is a bow but you do have a choice of size of loop and length of ends so don't be afraid to adjust these when you need to.

When tying a reef knot, remember this simple phrase: left over right, right over left.

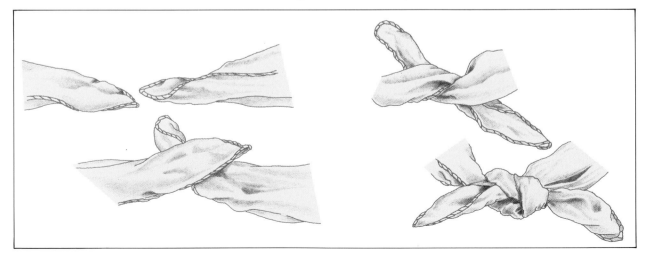

A basic turban is suitable for many occasions.

1 Position the middle of the scarf at the back of neck, in the center.

2 Bring two ends above head and cross them, pulling tightly.

3 Make another twist, and a third if you wish.

4 Pull all twists tight. Take ends to back of head and tuck them under bottom edge of turban.

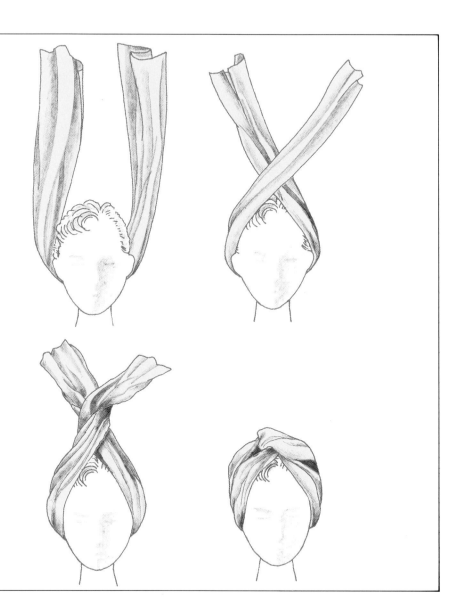

A BASIC TURBAN

It is useful to know how to make one of these as it can be appropriate for all kinds of occasions. You can add a wide-brimmed hat or decorate it with more scarves.

Start with a long rectangular scarf or fold a square diagonally and then into a strip. If you have long hair pin it up out of the way. With the middle of the scarf at the center back of your neck bring the two ends up above head, covering head with fabric. Cross the ends and pull tightly so that fabric is close to the head. Make another twist in the same way and a third one if you like; this depend on the length and thickness of the scarf. Pull all twists tight and take ends down to back of head, tucking ends in under bottom edge of turban. If the ends are not long enough to reach the bottom, tuck them in among the folds on top.

ACCESSORIES

You need very few extra bits and pieces to make scarf arrangements, but there are a few items which can be essential. Brooches and pins for holding scarves in place are certainly useful to have. A kilt pin looks fun used in the same way.

You can buy special scarf rings or use your own large size finger rings (nothing too precious) or small gilt or silver curtain rings. Discreet hair pins or hair grips are needed sometimes as an insurance against silk scarves slipping. It is possible to buy small self adhesive pads which grip to each other. If you gently press one on to one part of a scarf and its partner on another you can hold two edges in place with nothing showing.

Use jewelery in conjunction with scarves, winding and twisting them together or threading scarves through the links on chains or bracelets.

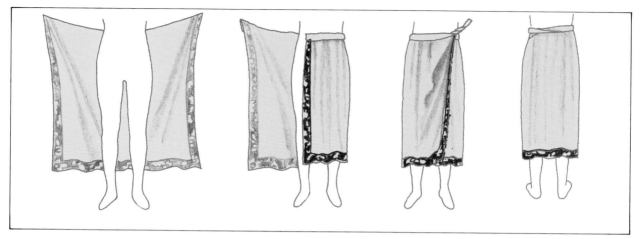

A sarong is exotic and fun.
1 Take the fabric and hold it behind you.
2 Fold top edge down over itself to make a waistband. Bring one top corner round to front of body.
3 Bring other side over, trapping first corner. Twirl free corner to make long, thin rope.
4 Take rope round to back of waist and tuck it into folds of fabric.

A SARONG SKIRT

Wonderful large colorful squares of fabric are available everywhere now to make wraps for tops, shoulders or hips. Take the piece of fabric and hold it behind you. Fold top edge down over itself to make a waistband. Bring one top corner round to front and across body. Bring other side over, trapping first corner. Twirl free corner to make a long, thin rope. Take this right round to back of waist and tuck it into folds of fabric at waist. Twirling the second end makes the front edge shorter and gives shape to the final skirt.

Make a few folds or pleats vertically in the sarong as you wrap it if you want greater ease of movement.

SCARF CARE

When you buy a new scarf it should be labeled to explain what fabric it is made from and how to care for it. Expensive silk scarves are always worth having professionally dry cleaned but cotton squares and man-made fabrics can simply be washed gently. To be safe if you are not sure how the scarf is printed or dyed then hand wash in warm water and line dry, finishing with a press with a warm iron. Wool scarves are best dry cleaned unless the care label says that hand washing is possible. Keep all scarves fresh by laundering or cleaning. Worn next to the skin or outside a garment which is worn in a grimy city, scarves quickly lose a pristine appearance and nothing looks quite as unattractive as a grubby scarf. Some dry cleaners will only take several scarves at a time to be cleaned and a few will not even be bothered with scarves at all. If you find a good and willing cleaners then stick to them and make a regular habit of having scarves freshened up so that they are always ready when you need them.

MAKING THE MOST OF WHAT YOU'VE GOT

A small collection of scarves can turn two outfits into twenty. Fashions come and go but a scarf stays the same. You will find that an old scarf you had hidden away is just the thing to finish off some new garment you've bought. Conversely an old outfit can be completely transformed by teaming a new scarf with it. Never underestimate the possibilities that a scarf gives to fashion. You can add a particular accent with a single knot; for example, a large soft scarf bow worn low over a blouse is romantic and old fashioned. A scarf tied tightly bandana style low over the forehead gives a tough masculine look; a floral shawl and frilled skirt suggests camp fires and gypsy dancing.

The off-beat and unexpected mixing of scarf with clothes is a useful device. Try using a highly patterned floral scarf combined with a neat, strict geometric patterned dress or jacket. Imagine a scarf covered with bold pink and red roses against a charcoal grey and white houndstoosh check jacket, or a richly colored ethnic print scarf with a fine narrow striped dress. The same idea somehow doesn't work in reverse so keep the smaller area of fabric, which is the scarf, in the extravagant design and the larger area, the dress or jacket, in the understated fabric.

Mixing patterned scarves together is another way to make more of what you've got. There should be some link between different designs either through color or pattern or even the texture of fabrics put together. Two scarves used together would need to be similar to look good but as you increase the number this does not seem to be so important.

Different sizes of floral patterns look good together and so do classic motifs and spots put with stripes and checks. Several plain colors can be twisted together or wrapped round each other; for example, three soft angora and wool winter scarves in pale sorbet solors of pink, peach and banana or a hotter mixture of brilliant red, shocking pink and purple.

Scarves and accessories are usually very carefully chosen and used in fashion pictures, both editorially and in advertisements. When you see a clever idea or a color scheme worth copying in a magazine or newspaper cut it out and make a file full of ideas. Just having gone to the trouble of doing this usually makes you remember the idea that inspired you. Once you start to look out for inspiration you will probably find it everywhere, from people on the street, fashions in films and on television, to travel brochures and music videos. Some of the specialist stores selling scarves have shows giving lots of ways of using scarves and some produce leaflets and brochures with hints on tying scarves and new ways to wear them.

Take care when putting scarves with clothes. Consider the different textures together and how well they relate. Contrast is usually successful but sometimes a scarf and dress of the same material is a better choice. Look carefully at photographs in fashion magazines. Learn what looks good and experiment with what might suit your own personal style. Above all, have fun and try all the ideas in this book. You may think that some of them will never work for you, but you will probably be pleasantly surprised. And, remember, none of them take longer than five minutes.

1
HEADS FIRST

SIMPLE DOUBLE-KNOT TURBAN

What you need
A rectangular scarf.

A very simple idea which is quick and easy to make and looks more relaxed and casual than the sophisticated version of a turban. A wide band like this can be worn in the same way over much longer hair or the hair can be tied or tucked up out of the way. Worn with loose hair the scarf would look like a very wide head band.

This scarf has a very pretty pattern made from blocks of different colors which are shown off well in this arrangement. Any type of scarf would work well, but the small tassels on this one add a very special touch.

To change the idea further, use a longer scarf and tie a bow on a single knot. It may take more courage to wear but would look stunning made in the right fabric. To make an ordinary knot look more substantial, make a couple of twists in the fabric after tying the first knot then tie the second knot and one final one to secure it all safely.

1 *If your scarf is too wide fold along its length to a width of about 9 inches (23 cm). Hold the ends tightly in both hands.*

2 *With center of scarf at middle of back of neck, wrap fabric under hair and bring to top of head. Finish with a double knot or bow.*

DRAPED SCARF AND WINTER HAT

What you need
One long, thin scarf
approximately 20
inches (50 cm) wide and
60 inches (150 cm)
long.
One simple winter hat

A glamorous yet very practical idea for winter weather. The scarf should be long enough to wrap over the head and cross at the front of the neck before dropping the ends down the back. If these are long enough they will stay in place.

Choose a fairly lightweight scarf in chiffon or silk so that it is not too bulky under the hat. It should also have a good drape so that it falls in flattering folds around the face.

Here the contrast of a severely shaped hat with an exotic print scarf is very dramatic. You could also arrange the scarf with a brimmed hat for an entirely different effect or try a summer version using a straw hat and a transparent, floaty scarf in a floral print. Choose the hat with care. It should be quite large and eye-catching so that the scarf is seen as the accessory and not the main garment.

1 *Choose a long, thin scarf which fits well under a simple winter hat*

2 *With center of scarf at the middle of your head, take both ends to back crossing one over other.*

3 *Let ends fall straight down back from each shoulder.*

THE CLASSIC WRAP

What you need
One large silk scarf approximately 36 inches (90 cm) square

This simple and feminine idea has been around for decades but never seems to date. It has a strong hint of the 1950s to it but can still look utterly up to the minute. Far more flattering than the under-the-chin knot version, this classic looks great with masculine trench coats or soft cashmere sweaters. In lighter weight fabrics it can be used in other seasons. On days when you want to be inconspicuous, just turn up your collar and add some shades.

You will need a square scarf that is large enough to allow ends to be taken back and tied behind the neck. The triangle of scarf at the back is caught under the knot and can be left outside a coat or tucked neatly away. Most commonly made using a silk scarf, this idea can also be successful using soft wool weaves. Avoid very large prints or border designs and go for classic spots, stripes, small-scale prints or plain colors.

1 *Fold square into a triangle. Put it over head and cross ends just framing the face and chin.*

2 *Take ends to back. Tie in a knot at back over points.*

3 *Tuck pointed ends inside coat at back or leave them free if you prefer.*

Classic scarf with romantic bow

What you need

A long, rectangular scarf approximately 30 inches (75 cm) wide and 90 inches (225 cm) long or a large scarf approximately 55 inches (140 cm) square.

This scarf arrangement is perfect for giving a dressier feel to the ordinary version of the same idea which has a simple knot at either the front or back. The soft bow is very decorative and can be made as large or as small as you want. You can have the two loops and two ends equal in length or the ends can be pulled very short to make much longer loops.

It looks good with a V-shaped neckline or simple round-necked dress. Avoid putting it with a dress or coat which has very fussy detail at the front as the two will clash. It is an excellent way to show off a really beautiful scarf as so much of the fabric is on view. Soft chiffon or fluid silk fabrics are best because they are full without being bulky. Fine woven wools such as challis would also work but avoid materials like cotton which are too stiff. The bow should be generous yet floppy and romantic. When you no longer need the scarf over your head simply drop it down to make a folded collar round your neck.

1 *If square, fold scarf into a triangle. With middle of front edge at center of head, put scarf over head.*

2 *Cross ends over each other at front of neck and take to back. Cross ends at back and bring them both forward.*

3 *Loosely tie a single knot and then make a bow. Spread the bow out and adjust length of loops and ends.*

BERET AND BANDANA

What you need
A square headscarf
A black wool beret

A brilliantly quick and easy way to transform a basic black beret, the scarf is tied over the head bandana-style and the beret simply put on top leaving a strip of scarf showing at the front. You can tuck hair up and out of the way but this arrangement probably works best with medium-length hair showing beneath the beret to soften the effect.

Any type of scarf can be put with the beret but something with strong, clear colors is necessary to establish the contrast since only a very small area of scarf is showing.

Once the ends of the scarf have been tied at the back and the beret is in place the loose ends can be tucked up inside the hat to give a slick finish. Leaving the ends loose and floating gives a different effect. Which you choose will probably depend on your hairstyle and the clothes you wear with the beret.

1 *If square, fold scarf into a triangle. Cover your head with scarf and take ends to back of neck.*

2 *Tie ends in small knot, pulling tightly to give a neat fit. Pull front edge down quite low over forehead before putting beret on top.*

DOUBLE-KNOT TURBAN

What you need
One very long scarf approximately 20 inches (50 cm) wide and 70 inches (175 cm) long.

At first glance this variation on a turban looks quite difficult to make. The trick is to use the stiffness of the fabric to achieve the look. To get the best from this idea choose a scarf made from cotton or a fabric with some body, such as silk taffetta, which will fold crisply and stay in place. The scarf must be long enough to wrap round the head and make a double knot.

This style looks best with a face line clear of hair. If you have long hair to hide, tuck it inside the scarf and pin it as flat as possible first to avoid lumps and bulges at the back. Bold but simple gold or silver earrings seem to be an important and natural accessory.

Choose the brightest and most dazzling fabrics you dare. The idea is a bold one so don't play it down with nondescript colors and wishy-washy patterns. Checks, spots, stripes and florals in strong colors will all look terrific.

1 With center of scarf at center of head cover head and hair with scarf and take ends to back.

2 Cross ends and bring up to top of head. Tie single knot at top of head.

3 Tie second knot slightly lower down head and fan out ends to make them stand proud.

2
NECK LINES

ROLL-NECK ROSES

What you need
A large scarf
approximately 36
inches (90 cm) square.

This is a very relaxed and pretty arrangement that makes a bold statement. The scarf is tied with points at the front and the folds of the fabric are pulled back over the knot like a big, soft roll neck. It is flattering to most people and can be worn in a casual way with denims and outdoor clothes or smartly by using a sophisticated silk square with a city suit or neat coat. It is best worn inside a shirt opening or collar of some kind.

Most kinds of square scarf would be suitable for this idea except one that is too thick and bulky. The soft cotton scarf shown is perfect, with full use made of the random-printed rose design.

1 *Fold square into a triangle. Hold the triangle in front of you and take the ends to back of neck.*

2 *Cross ends at back and bring them to front. Tie a neat knot about half way down triangle with fullness above the knot.*

3 *Pull the top edge of fabric down over knot and spread the collar slightly too.*

ROLLED KERCHIEF

What you need

A small cotton scarf or handkerchief approximately 18 inches (46 cm) square.

A small, neat cotton square rolled and tied quite tightly round the neck is a good way to finish off a casual kind of outfit or to add a dash of color or pattern to simple clothes.

Tied in a knot at the side of the neck it has a kind of raffish feel which is definitely a look for outdoors. Traditionally they were worn by women as a head-dress. These small cotton squares were also worn by nineteenth-century workmen and often came in simple spot and stripe designs in plain bright colors with white. This square has a slightly more subtle design but it still has a hint of the kerchief.

Rolling the scarf gives it a good shape, makes it more comfortable to wear and is far more flattering as a rounded tube than a flat folded scarf.

1 *Fold the square diagonally to make a triangle with wrong sides of fabric inside.*

2 *Lie the triangle on a flat surface and begin to roll it from the point towards the folded edge.*

3 *Put it round your neck with the edge against your neck and securely tie a double knot.*

CANDY-STRIPED CRAVAT

What you need

A rectangular scarf approximately 40 inches (100 cm) or a ready-made cravat.

Cravat scarves can be bought ready-made but usually only in traditional and rather masculine designs and colors. Pleated and shaped they are meant to be worn inside an open shirt collar. The shaping isn't strictly necessary so any straight scarf can be used to fill in a neck line stylishly. This idea plays with the stripe theme in a subtle way and the rather severe look of a man's cravat couldn't be sweeter than when it is made from pink and white candy stripes.

Made from a fabric which isn't too shiny the cravat should stay put quite well when the ends are tucked down inside a shirt. You could add a touch of sparkle with a discreeet tie pin or simple brooch which will also help to hold the ends in the right position. Try different versions with a paisley fabric and simple cream shirt, a striped cravat with a spotted shirt or vice versa. A cravat should be worn with the fold quite high up under the chin and only the top two shirt buttons left open.

1 Fold scarf fabric neatly to make about 5 inches (13 cm) width. Put scarf round neck and bring ends forward and make a single knot.

2 Twist the top layer to make one end lie flat over the other. Spread out fabric to give a neat, smooth line.

3 Tuck bottom end down into shirt then tuck upper end inside too.

WAISTCOAT TRANSFORMATION

What you need

A short, rectangular scarf approximately 15 inches (38 cm) wide and 36 inches (90 cm) long.

This kind of arrangement can transform an outfit and make it wearable in a totally different way. The waistcoat looks great under a jacket but it needs a filler-in at the neck. The scarf gives the illusion of a shirt and adds color and emphasis.

Concentrate on texture with an idea like this. The matt wool of the waistcoat looks superb with a scarf made from rich jewel-red shot silk which is shiny and alive with contrast. The same type of scarf would also look good used under a jacket worn without a shirt or a deep V-necked plain dress.

1 *With center of scarf at center of back of neck bring both ends to front.*

2 *Take one end and tuck it inside one edge of waistcoat.*

3 *Take other end and cross it over first end, also tucking edges under waistcoat.*

DRAPED, TWISTED AND PINNED

What you need
A very long scarf
approximately 75
inches (190 cm)
A brooch

A long, soft, flowing chiffon scarf looks wonderful but is often quite unpractical to wear. Here it is softly draped and twisted round the neck, the two ends discreetly held in place with a suitable brooch. When the scarf is fastened in this way you won't need to keep checking and re-wrapping it.

This arrangement looks good over a sweater or knitted dress and can be the means of adding shape and/or color to something very plain. It frames the neck and face prettily but still has some floating ends for fun.

Try using the same idea with a bigger, thicker outdoor type of scarf worn over a jacket or coat. The indoor version is really best with quite fine and soft fabrics such as chiffon.

1 *With middle of scarf at center front of neck take ends to back, cross them then bring ends to front.*

2 *Twist one end through and round neck loop once or twice.*

3 *Do the same with the other side until you have two manageable ends.*

4 *Take both ends across to one side and pin to dress with a brooch.*

THE BIG LOOP

What you need

Any warm neck scarf approximately 60 inches (150 cm) or longer.

The simplest ideas are often the most functional as this arrangement demonstrates. It's surprising how many people haven't discovered that the way to keep a winter scarf from flying away in the wind is to double it up and put the ends through the loop.

Fastened this way the scarf can be worn and forgotten about while continuing to be sleek and unfussy, with elegant coats as well as sporty clothes. Most woolen neck scarves are long enough to loop in this way but an especially big one will mean you can make a generous shape round the neck and still have plenty of length to spare.

Try using two scarves together by putting them side by side and treating them as if they were one.

1 *Fold scarf in half across width. With loop end in one hand and two loose ends in the other, wrap scarf round neck.*

2 *Push loose ends through the loop and pull to required tightness.*

CONTINENTAL LOOP

What you need
A classic silk square.

This is a sleek and sophisticated arrangement which will make the most of a beautiful silk square. It looks soft and pretty when made with a scarf that covers the shoulders, but the same idea can be used successfully with a smaller scarf too.

The scarf is simply fastened through a loop of the fabric, giving more definition and shape than is achieved by simply knotting the ends together. You can choose to a certain extent where you make the loop thus varying the lengths of the scarf ends and determining where the triangle sits. Experiment until you find the right position.

A patterned or strongly colored scarf will make a bold statement but you could also try this idea using a scarf and shirt of toning plain colors to achieve a very different effect.

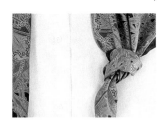

1 *Fold into a triangle. Drape round shoulders. Make a loose knot at one end, leaving 4 inches (10 cm) of fabric below it.*

2 *With opposite scarf edge make a small loop at about the same position as the first knot.*

3 *Pull the loop through the knot and then pull on knot to tighten it, trapping the loop.*

4 *Spread out the loop into a good shape. Adjust the whole scarf until it sits comfortably and looks right.*

3
SHOULDER
SHAPES

Bold Checks Under a Belt

What you need
A scarf 48 inches (122 cm) long
A wide belt

Another idea for changing the look of basic clothes, this time with the addition of a fringed woolen scarf. The strong check design adds pattern and texture to a monochrome outfit.

You could use the same idea by tucking the scarf inside a more formal jacket or choose a completely different scarf and add a bold splash of color. For a more glamorous feel you could use a silky scarf worn directly over the skin, eliminating the shirt.

The belt is the vital component, so choose it with care. It should be wide enough to stay fitting well and hold the scarf in the right position while allowing free movement. Link the scarf color with the belt color if possible for a well coordinated look.

1 *Drape the scarf down over the front of the body. Put the belt around it and re-arrange the scarf if necessary.*

2 *Put on jacket or cardigan and tuck bottom edges down under belt.*

STRIPED SHOULDER SASH

What you need
A long sash or scarf approximately 10 inches (25 cm) wide and 70 inches (175 cm) long.

If you own a beautiful scarf that deserves to be shown, try wearing it like a ceremonial sash across one shoulder. It produces quite a dressy effect which should be set off by very simple shapes underneath. A loose unstructured shirt or dress will look better than a clinging or fitting item of clothing.

The idea introduces a hint of ceremony and occasion, so resist adding lots of other accessories which might suggest fancy-dress. If you don't own a beautiful, embroidered heirloom or woven silk scarf then use a strip of any decorative fabric cut and hemmed to size.

1 *With the middle of the scarf at the shoulder, drape the fabric down across the body to opposite hip.*

2 *Tie a single knot if there is enough fabric or pin two ends together with a brooch.*

COUNTRY CLASSIC

What you need
A classic-design silk scarf
approximately 36
inches (90 cm) square.

We expect to see classic silk head squares tied to a handbag strap or firmly knotted under a chin at race meetings. Taken away from their cashmere and pearl environment they can look fresh, new and totally different. Try combining a boldly patterned scarf with low-key country clothes such as a tweed hacking jacket, cream silk shirt and jodphurs. Tied in a neat knot at the front the design is shown off beautifully on the triangle which lies across the back and shoulders.

To look its best the scarf must be immaculate and perfectly pressed and then it will do wonders for even the oldest of tweeds. Take care with the color scheme as some of the classic scarves have startling colour combinations; best to wear them with neutrals such as cream, beige and gray.

1 *Fold into a triangle with upper side showing slightly more than under side.*

2 *Drape the scarf over the back and shoulders. Tie ends at front into small double knot.*

BARE BACK AND BOW

What you need

A scarf approximately 20 inches (50 cm) wide and 75 inches (190 cm) long.

An instant top for sunny days. If you choose to make this idea with bright cotton and wild prints then it is perfect for the beach and garden. Worn with a sarong it would make a cool outfit for hot, sticky days.

In a very different mood the same arrangement could be made for evening using a soft chiffon or silk scarf to wear with wide trousers or long, draped sarong shaped skirt. It could also look stunning worn under an evening jacket so that just the folded fabric showed at the front. For a more enclosed look a wide cummerbund sash could cover the midriff.

You can vary this arrangement slightly by wrapping the scarf round the neck, crossing it then tying it behind the waist. This works well with a stretchy knitted fabric scarf.

1 *With the middle of the scarf at the center of the lower back bring the scarf forward.*

2 *Cross the scarf at the front and pull tightly up to the neck.*

3 *Tie the scarf ends behind your neck into a double knot. Tighten or loosen knot for comfort.*

SHOULDERS ON SHOW

What you need

A scarf approximately 36 inches (90 cm) square.

Made from clean blue, gray and white over a lace-edged peasant blouse this off-the-shoulder scarf has a sweet and innocent look about it. Try the arrangement using a bright floral on a dark background style of scarf or plain and simple polka dots on a deep color. While it could be worn over a normal sleeved shirt the whole point is to show off the shoulders. A simple black or white scoop-necked T-shirt with enough stretch to pull down on to the arms would also look good under the scarf. Wear a flouncy skirt, summer shorts or neat tapered 1950s style trousers for maximum effect. Add a beret and look very Left Bank.

1 *If scarf is square, fold into a triangle. With scarf at center back bring end forward, wrapping upper arms.*

2 *Tie at center front in a small double knot or bow. Adjust height of scarf and blouse for comfort.*

THE WINTER WRAP

What you need
A large woolen scarf at least 60 inches (150 cm) square.

A big sweep of shawl is a marvelous way of adding some color and style to a warm and practical winter coat or raincoat. For years scarves were worn discreetly tucked inside a collar, but they are now worn over coats to provide swirl and panache on the streets.

The scarf will stay in place if it's a non-shiny textured fabric such as a fine wool or wool mixture. If it is big enough its weight alone will help hold it in place. If you are frightened it might slide, then you can always hold it on the shoulder with a very small pin or a brooch of a suitable design.

A large scarf looks wonderful made from a fabric with lots of movement in the pattern – border prints are really shown off to their best in large scarves. Choose from subtle florals, rich paisleys or clever geometric designs.

1 Fold square into a triangle. Hold it behind your back with the bottom point just inside the right elbow.

2 Lie the left-hand point down, covering the arm. Sweep right-hand point across front of body.

3 Let the point fall down over the left shoulder. Adjust the whole wrap to make it comfortable and wearable.

4
WAISTS AND
HIPS

SILK PARTY SASH

What you need
A silk scarf
approximately 10
inches (25 cm) wide and
65 inches (165 cm)
long.

Make a simple shirt and skirt into a party dress with a sash made from a silk scarf. In times past a plain white dress was enlivened at each wearing by a different colored party sash. In much the same way you can lift a dress or skirt out of the ordinary by using scarves you already have.

Make a bold statement with contrasting strong colors. Here the brilliant shocking pink looks beautiful against charcoal grey. Move the knot to wherever it looks best and change the proportion of loop to ends to find what suits you. A stiffish fabric with some body is necessary so that the knot is generous and as full as possible. A soft fabric will simply hang limply. Plain colors possess maximum impact, but a vertical or diagonal stripe could look stunning.

1 With middle of scarf at center of back, bring ends forward. Tie a single knot to a comfortable tightness.

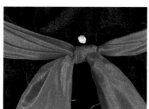

2 Tie a second knot so that scarf is secure.

3 With one end make a loose knot about half way along its length. Fold the other end in half across the width.

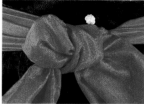

4 Push the loop through loose knot, tighten knot and pull loop through, spreading out the fabric.

Draped dhoti

What you need
A large length of fabric or sarong approximately 40 inches (100 cm) wide and 80 inches (200 cm) long.

Some of the most stylish clothes are made from pieces of fabric wrapped and tied round the body. All over the world there are examples of such ingeneous garments which require neither sewing nor cutting.

From togas to saris and sarongs there are rich influences to take ideas from, and because these clothes really have to be functional they seem invariably to look wonderful as well.

If you buy lengths of interesting fabrics when abroad use them in these simple ways. Very often wrapping them rather than constructing with them actually shows off their beautiful designs and prints to better advantage.

1 *Take two corners at the top of the piece of fabric around the waist and tie in a double knot at back.*

2 *Pick up the remaining two corners and bring ends up behind you through legs.*

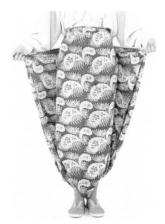

3 *Bring the two ends round to the front of the waist.*

4 *Tie the corners together just below the stomach. This gives a more attractive line as well as ease of movement.*

DIAGONAL DRAPE

What you need
A large scarf
approximately 45
inches (115 cm) square.

Belts often provide the finishing touch that is needed for separates. A fabric belt can do more than add an accent. It can pull two pieces of clothing together by adding emphasis and shape where needed, subtly turning them into a complete outfit. A scarf tied tightly on the hips can define and flatten a waist, put some shape into a full gathered skirt or emphasize the slinkiness of a narrow one.

This ethnic scarf gives texture and curves to a straightforward mix of separates and wrapped on the diagonal is easier to wear and more stylish than a straight wide band. If the scarf is large you can tie the ends on the hip with the point; if it is small just fasten it on the opposite hip.

1 If you have a triangular scarf, use it as it is.

2 If not, simply fold a large square diagonally across to make a triangle.

3 With lower pointed corner at side of hip, wrap scarf ends across body. Cross on opposite hip and bring ends back to first hip.

4 Tie ends into a double knot and tuck out of sight in folds which will have naturally appeared.

DOUBLE SCARF BELT

What you need
Two small cotton scarves approximately 18 inches (45 cm) square.

The idea of using a scarf as a belt for jeans has been around for quite a while. This version makes use of bandanas or handkerchiefs which everyone seems to have tucked at the back of a drawer. The red and blue spotted kerchiefs here are similar in style to each other, but there is no reason why you shouldn't mix colors and patterns to produce all kinds of different effects. Most colors look good with faded denims but keep to small-scale prints and patterns as such a small area of scarf shows at any one time.

You can also braid scarves together for another version of this idea. Again, if they are short they can simply be joined where necessary. You will need three used together for a proper braid but you could simply twist two together. The limiting factor is the width of belt carrier on your jeans, so experiment with scarves of different fabrics and thicknesses.

1 *The two scarves should be the same size if possible. Roll or fold each scarf into a neat shape with loose edge underneath.*

2 *Join the two scarves together with a small neat double knot.*

3 *Thread the belt through the belt carriers with the loose edge against the fabric.*

4 *Tie a double knot at the front of the jeans. The joining knot should be at the center back.*

KNOTTED SCARF BEACH BAG

What you need
A large scarf
  approximately 60
  inches (150 cm) square.

Faced with having to carry several things and with no obvious means of doing so no doubt many people have worked out a make-shift bag from a square of material. It is the ultimate lightweight luggage and a perfect answer to the problem of carrying books, sun tan lotion and refreshments down to the beach or pool. You need a square scarf made from anything but the flimsiest of fabrics. Obviously it isn't sensible to carry very sharp or awkwardly shaped things in your best silk chiffon head square but the resulting bag is tough and flexible; it is pretty stylish too, especially if you co-ordinate it with a swimsuit and sarong.

The basic sarong pictured here can be tied by following the instructions found on page 12 in the Five-Minute Approach.

1 *Lie the square on the floor or a table and put what you want to carry inside.*

2 *Take two diagonal corners into the middle and tie together quite tightly in a double knot.*

3 *Take the other two corners and tie at their very ends to give a long shoulder strap for carrying.*

5
DAZZLING
DECORATIONS

CHIFFON JEWELS

What you need
A small scarf of chiffon
  or very fine fabric
  which forms soft folds.
A brooch.

A scarf doesn't have to be practical and it doesn't always have to be wrapped or tied round a part of the body. Scarves can be crumpled and twisted, pleated and rolled into shapes to attach to clothes or hats. In this way they can be used as if they were jewels – items you add to a garment for an accent of color or as a means of drawing attention to a line or detail.

In this arrangement a small chiffon scarf has been bunched into a soft rosette and a brooch used to attach it to a jacket. You could also make a collection of smaller jewels to wear in a group or you could pin one colored scarf rosette against a different colored one. If you first fold the scarf into a flat strip then wrap it round itself you can create scarf flowers which can be attached to a jacket by means of a brooch in the same way.

1 *Bring edges into the middle, holding them in one hand. Crumple into a small round shape, keeping all the· edges on one side.*

2 *Holding the scarf together transfer to jacket with edges at back. Pin to jacket with brooch.*

EXOTIC EVENING TURBAN

What you need
A selection of small
  chiffon scarves to tone
  with turban.
Pins.

A turban is a wonderful way of creating great style
and at the same time hiding hair that's not quite up
to the occasion. It isn't only for the brave few – a
scarf turban can be surprisingly flattering to all ages
and face shapes. It must look extravagant and the
color should be chosen with care to suit your skin
type. The instructions for making a basic turban are
on page 10.

Here the basic turban has been improved upon
with soft rosettes made from small silk and chiffon
scarves which tone with the burnt orange of the
turban and add spicy colors to the exotic mixture.
Pin them in place after you have put the turban on
and aim for a slightly asymmetric arrangement
which gives some extra height to the head; three to
five is probably the right number.

1 *Fold each small chiffon
scarf into an envelope
shape, bringing each corner
into the middle.*

2 *Bring the new corners into
the middle in the same way.*

3 *Now scrunch scarf
together to make a rosette.
Use pins in the center to hold
it together.*

4 *Attach rosettes singly to
turban with pins or safety
pins.*

HANDKERCHIEF BANGLES

What you need
Small scarves
approximately 18
inches (45 cm) square.

This is a very quick way to jazz up a plain outfit with color and pattern. Small handkerchief-sized scarves are folded into bands and tied round the wrist. You can mix and match different designs in the same color range as here or have fun with lots of different colors. You can afford to clash when there is such a small amount of each one showing.

Floating chiffon scarves could look pretty too or the fabric bangles could be mixed with an armful of real jewelery threaded between and among the scarves. It is possible to tie these on yourself, but it is even quicker if you ask a friend to help.

1 *Fold squares into triangles. Roll up from the point to the long edge.*

2 *Tie each one into a single knot.*

3 *Tie a double knot if fabric is likely to spring apart.*

BRAIDED RIBBON AND SCARVES

What you need

Two chiffon scarves approximately 36 inches (90 cm) long.
A length of ribbon approximately 36 inches (90 cm) long.

A stunning woven braid made from two chiffon scarves and a length of ribbon. Three scarves together would become very bulky so by using a flat strip of ribbon you have the third strip to braid properly which takes up very little space.

You can have fun choosing scarves to make this arrangement. The ribbon color can be the link between two quite different styles of scarf but make sure that the three colors are contrasting to get the best effect.

The finished braid could also be worn as a headband with long hair, either low over the forehead or further back and tucked over or behind the ears. A long braid like this could be worn as a belt or sash or even round the neck as a dramatic necklace. Make the braid on a flat surface and stand something heavy on the three ends to hold them as you begin to work.

1 *Choose the scarves and ribbon of roughly the same length. Lie them on a flat surface and begin to braid.*

2 *Continue keeping tension as equal as possible. Wrap round hair and tie ends in a double knot. Pin in place.*

PAISLEY SCARF CHIGNON

What you need
A scarf approximately
   27 inches (68 cm)
   square.

A very soft and pretty way to wrap a chignon of hair for a daytime look. You do need a good-sized chignon to begin with but by tying a knot or two in the scarf and turning this to the inside you can add the illusion of more hair than there really is.

Using a scarf with a border that is different to the main part of the square will provide you with a contrasting bow against the chignon. Most people who have long hair seem to manage dressing it without being able to see what they are doing so tying this idea should not be very difficult. Check in a mirror that the bow is horizontal and the loops are equal.

1 *Tie a knot or two in the center of the square on the inside of the fabric.*

2 *Take two diagonal ends and pull scarf to a long strip. Wrap center of strip under hair, covering the hair and supporting it with scarf.*

3 *Bring ends to top and tie into a single knot, catching the top edge of the scarf under it.*

4 *Tie scarf ends into a bow and spread loops to make them as equal and broad as possible. The center knot should not be too tight.*

SILK WRAPPED EVENING CHIGNON

What you need

A small scarf approximately 24 inches (60 cm) square.

A very simple hair decoration for a special evening which looks complicated and elaborate. A small silk scarf is tied in a knot then wound round a pony tail of hair. It is successful with even quite short hair tied back, as the fullness of the scarf compensates for any lack of hair. If you have very full hair, pin it up into a sleek bun or chignon before wrapping the scarf.

Choose a strongly-colored scarf such as fuchsia pink, strident red or deep forest green. The color here is linked to the chiffon bow at the back of the dress. Copy the bow idea by tying a long scarf into a large looped bow and pin or stitch to the dress.

It is perfectly possible to make the hair decoration oneself as the wrapping is quite random. Check in a mirror or ask someone to see that the ends are tucked away neatly when you are finished. Grip the scarf with small hair pins to be sure it stays in place all evening.

1 Fold a square scarf to make a triangle and then a strip. Tie it round secured pony 'ail and fasten with a single knot.

2 Using both hands bring ends down and round hair then up again. Continue to cross scarf once or twice, swapping hands as you go.

3 Tie a small knot underneath hair and tuck the loose ends out of sight. Pin scarf to hair with hair pins if you like.

KNOTS AND CHAINS

What you need

A long, narrow scarf
approximately 50
inches (125 cm).
Two or more chains or
necklaces.

A series of knots can transform a transparent black and gold scarf into an evening necklace. Twisted with gold chains and worn with pearls, no one would imagine it could be put together in a few minutes.

With this arrangement after tying a couple of knots you'll quickly discover how far along the scarf you need to be before you start making the next one. Have a trial run to set out the spacing between the knots. This decision will depend on the thickness of the fabric of the scarf and what kind of jewelery you wish to twine through the necklace.

For another idea, a longer scarf could be knotted all along its length and worn as a belt or the long ends of a sash could be knotted in graduated sizes from largest at the bottom working upwards to smallest at the top.

1 *Tie a knot at one end, leaving enough scarf to tie with other side eventually.*

2 *Continue along the scarf, tying single loose large knots. Carry on till you have enough to fit neck.*

3 *Finally, wrap and twist the two chains round the spaces between the knots. Tie scarf round neck and fasten chains.*

INDEX

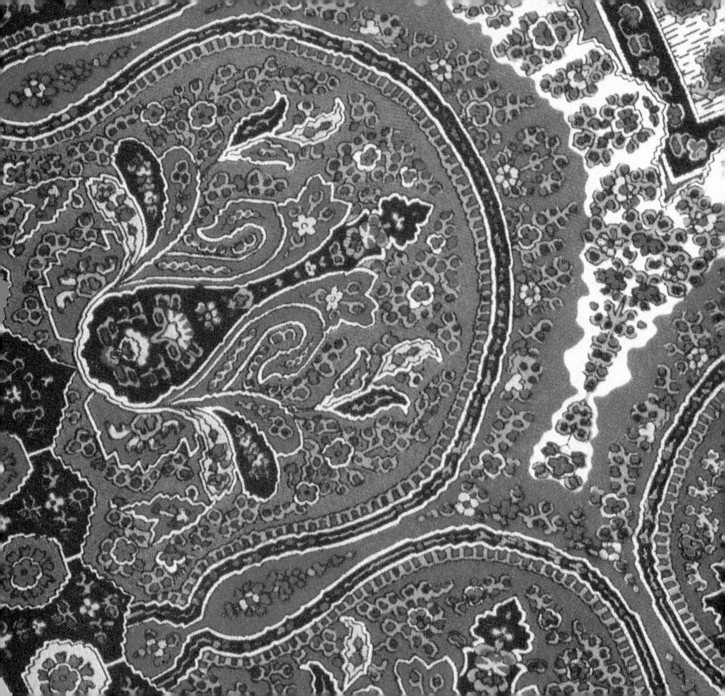